W9-APO-973

Haiku

宮島

*gateway to a shrine
in an inland sea at Miyajima*

HAIKU

Gems of Intimate Beauty In a New

Collection of Classic Japanese Poetry

Selected by Mary Dawson Hughes

 HALLMARK EDITIONS

'Three Lines Are Enough'

Reporting back from Japan some years ago, the Nobel-Prize-winning Indian author Rabindranath Tagore had this to say about the poetic form called *haiku:*

"Often a poem consists of no more than three lines, but these are sufficient both for poets and readers. That is why I have never heard anyone singing in the streets since I have been here. The hearts of these people are not resonant like a waterfall, but silent like a lake. All their poems which I have heard are picture-poems, not song-poems. When the heart aches and burns, then life is spent; the Japanese spend very little in this direction. Their inner self finds complete expression in their sense of beauty, which is independent of self-interest. We do not have to break our hearts over flowers and birds or the moon. Our only connection with them is the enjoyment of beauty; they do not hurt us anywhere, or deprive us of anything; our lives are in no wise maimed by them. That is why three lines are enough."

Tagore was right in his reaction to *haiku,* though not all these brief poems spare us

3

strong emotions. But they glance, and turn away to think. *Haiku* never stare.

The best way to read a *haiku* is to return to it several times, each time allowing yourself leisure to visualize the scene it depicts, the feelings it dramatizes, the situation of the speaker—and then simply daydream. For *haiku* depend on the reader to fill in with detail the settings they sketch.

Basho, Buson, and Issa appear often in this book. They are Japan's three best-known *haiku* poets. Basho (1644-1694) was a religious man, a poet who found God in nature. Buson (1715-1783), an artist, dealt with existing things in their concrete immediacy—the here and now. Issa (1763-1827) was a humanist, concerned with man, birds and beasts in their struggle for survival. Each poet brings to the brief concentration of his *haiku* his own expansive point of view.

"There is not only brevity of wording in these poems," continues Tagore, "there is also brevity of feeling which is not disturbed by the heart's emotion; it may be called the heart's economy. I think there is something deeply symbolical of Japan in this."

Introduction   3
'A Heavy Fall of Snow'   7
'The Waters of Spring'   19
'Under the Summer Moon'   35
'Entering Autumn'   47

The wren is chirruping,
But it grows dusk
Just the same.
ISSA

How beautiful
The usually hateful crow,
This morn of snow!
BASHO

Hail,
Flying into the fire
As fast as its legs can carry it.
ISSA

富士と霧氷・忍野村

a view of Mt. Fuji in winter

While the fowls
Were asleep,—
   A heavy fall of snow.
           KIEN

Winter moonlight;
The shadow of the stone pagoda,
   The shadow of the pine-tree.
           SHIKI

Rain blows
Into the bamboo forest;
   Evening.
           SEISEI

My bones
Feel the quilts;
   A frosty night.
           BUSON

Cold winter rain;
Mingling their horns,
    The oxen of the moor.
                    RANKO

The flame is motionless,
A rounded sphere
    Of winter seclusion.
                    YAHA

Cleaning a saucepan,—
Ripples on the water:
    A solitary sea-gull.
                    BUSON

White chrysanthemums,
Yellow chysanthemums,
    Would there were no other names!
                    RANSETSU

Even the storm of breath
Is white,
This winter morn.
SHO-I

The winter night;
Without any reason,
I listen to my neighbor.
KIKAKU

The winter moon:
A temple without a gate,—
How high the sky!
BUSON

The winter storm,
The voice of the rushing water,
Torn by the rocks.
BUSON

The Great Morning:
Winds of long ago
Blow through the pine tree.
ONITSURA

The setting sun,
Behind the eagle's nest,
In the boughs of the camphor-tree.
BONCHO

The moon beginning to fall
On four or five people,
Dancing!
BUSON

Day is dawning;
The voices of wild ducks
Are surrounding the castle.
KYOROKU

浅間神社

snow-covered lanterns on the grounds of the Asama Shrine

New Year's Day:
The sky is cloudless;
Sparrows are gossiping.

RANSETSU

The winter river;
Down it come floating
Flowers offered to Buddha.

BUSON

The wintry grove,
Echoes
Of long, long ago.

ISSA

Walking in the winter rain,
The umbrella
Pushes me back.

SHISEIJO

14

The first snow;
Beyond the sea,
    What mountains are they?
        SHIKI

A pool,
Deep in the forest;
    The ice is thick.
        SHIKI

The moon at daybreak
The plovers of the shore
    Vanishing far away.
        CHORA

To wake, alive, in this world,
What happiness!
    Winter rain.
        SHOHA

The storm has come:
The empty shell
Of a snail.
SOSHI

As one of us,
The cat is seated here;
The parting year.
ISSA

A solitary bird
For my companion
Upon the withered moor.
SENNA

The old man of the temple,
Splitting wood
In the winter moonlight.
BUSON

When I think it is my snow
On my hat,
  It seems light.
            KIKAKU

Loneliness;
After the fireworks,
  A falling star.
            SHIKI

On horseback;
My shadow
  Creeps freezing below.
            BASHO

Companionless,
Thrown away on the moor,
  The winter moon.
            ROSEKI

'The Waters of Spring'

The dawn of day;
On the tip of the barley leaf
The frost of spring.

ONITSURA

The spring breeze;
Through the barley,
The sound of waters.

MOKUDO

Spring rain;
The river willows blow back
The straw-coats.

BASHO

19

桜と松本城・長野

cherry blossoms on the grounds
of Matsumoto Castle at Nagano

In places without names,
Gladsome and lovely
    Wild cherry-blossoms.
                KOSHUN

The skylark singing
Ripples
    The clouds.
                SEIEN

Ranged along
The hand-rail around the corridor,
    The mountains of spring.
                SHIKI

The wild cherry:
Stones also are singing their songs
    In the valley stream.
                ONITSURA

In my hut this spring,
There is nothing,—
    There is everything!
                    SODO

The whitebait,—
As though the color of the water
    Were moving.
                    RAIZAN

The fawn
Shakes off the butterfly,
    And sleeps again.
                    ISSA

The song of the bird!
But the plum-tree in the grove
    Is not yet blooming.
                    ISSA

With the melting of the snow,
The village
    Frees the ponies.
            SHIKI

Treading on the bridge,
The fishes sink out of sight:
    The spring water.
            SHIKI

Mice in their nest
Squeak in response
    To the young sparrows.
            BUSHO

The kitten,
Weighed on the balance,
    Is still playing.
            ISSA

The setting sun
Treads on the tail
    Of the copper pheasant.
        BUSON

A basket of grass,
And no one there,—
    Mountains of spring.
        SHIKI

The quarrel
In the ale-house,
    Revived by the hazy moon.
        SHIKI

Not knowing
It is a famous place,
    A man hoeing the field.
        SHIKI

The bell from far away,—
How it moves along in its coming
    Through the spring haze!
        ONITSURA

The peacock,
Spreading out his tail
    In the spring breeze.
        SHIKI

The puppy asleep,
Biting
    The willow-tree.
        ISSA

With every falling petal,
The plum branches
    Grow older.
        BUSON

A world of grief and pain,
Even when cherry-blossoms
Have bloomed.
                    ISSA

It sticks like butter
To everything,—
This spring snow.
                    ISSA

The plum-blossoms falling,
Mother of pearl
Is spilt on the table.
                    BUSON

The lights are lit
On the islands far and near:
The spring sea.
                    SHIKI

Now making friends
Now scared of people,—
    The baby sparrow.
                ONITSURA

Pipe in mouth,
Mr. Boatman:
    The spring breeze!
                BASHO

Suddenly thinking of it
I went out and was sweeping the garden;
    A spring evening.
                TAIRO

A spring breeze this morning:
A shop that sells kites
    Has opened.
                SHOHA

At the passing of the boat,
Beating on the shore,
    The waters of spring.
                    TAIGI

The soft breeze,
And in the green of a thousand hills,
    A single temple.
                    SHIKI

The temple bell dies away.
The scent of flowers in the evening
    Is still tolling the bell.
                    BASHO

On the road-side,
Spilled from someone's hand,
    Flowers of buckwheat.
                    BUSON

奈良の池

a small lake in Nara

At dawn,
Coming up in the well-bucket,
   A camellia flower.
                    KAKEI

Tilling the field:
The cloud that never moved
   Is gone.
                    BUSON

Placing his hands on the ground,
The frog respectfully recites
   His poem.
                    SOKAN

Where the cliff has broken down,
Small fish gather,
   Under the river willow.
                    SHIKI

All the evening the only sound,
The falling
   Of the white camellia flowers.
           RANKO

In the warmth,
The white house-walls
   Ranged along the creek.
           SHIKI

As the swallow flies to and fro,
Its shadow is cast
   Upon the old door.
           SHOHA

Tilling the field;
My house also is seen
   As evening falls.
           BUSON

Spring rain;
Rain-drops from the willow,
Petals from the plum-tree.
SHOHA

On the sandy beach,
Footprints:
Long is the spring day.
SHIKI

This day on which
The cherry blossoms fell,
Has drawn to its close.
CHORA

Where the spring sun
Sinks down,—
The wistaria flowers.
ISSA

Heat-waves;
Petals of the plum flutter down
   Onto the stones.
                    SHIKI

Reluctantly
The willow leaves the boat
   Far behind.
                    KITO

Ah, singing skylark!
The tail-end of the grove
   Is still in darkness.
                    ISSA

With that voice,
Give us a little dance,
   Croaking frog!
                    ISSA

'Under the Summer Moon'

The summer rains
Will return Mount Fuji
Into the lake?

BUSON

On the faces of the cormorants
Splash waves,
Glittering with light.

CHORA

A red morning sky
For you, snail;
Are you glad about it?

ISSA

中禅寺湖畔、雨後の傘干し

*parasols drying after
a rain at Lake Chuzenji*

I sit here
Making the coolness
    My dwelling place.
            BASHO

The cool breeze
Fills the empty vault of heaven
    With the voice of the pine-tree.
            ONITSURA

Huge trees are many,
Their names unknown:
    The voices of the cicadas.
            SHIKI

Under the evening moon,
The snail
    Is stripped to the waist.
            ISSA

Moonlight slants through
The vast bamboo grove:
    A cuckoo cries.
            BASHO

The foal
Sticks out his nose
    Over the irises.
            ISSA

From out of the darkness
Of the short night
    Comes the River Oi.
            BUSON

In the summer rain,
The leaves of the plum-tree
    Are the color of the chill breeze.
            SAIMARO

The short night;
In the shallows remains
The crescent moon.
                BUSON

The kingfisher;
On its wet feathers
Shines the evening sun.
                TORI

My hermitage
Is thatched
With morning-glories.
                ISSA

Round the small house
Struck by lightning,
Melon-flowers.
                BUSON

The drum resounds
In the shrine yonder in the fields,
White clouds piled high.
HOKUSHI

Peeping through
The willow, lonely
With stars.
CHORA

The fan-seller;
A load of wind he carries,—
Ah, the heat!
KAKO

A sudden summer shower;
The village sparrows
Hang on to the grasses.
BUSON

名古屋近郊の寺

a temple on the outskirts of Nagoya

The voices of village people
Irrigating the fields;
   The summer moon.
            BUSON

She has put the child to sleep,
And now washes the clothes;
   The summer moon.
            ISSA

All the fishermen of the beach
Are away;
   The poppies are blooming.
            KYORAI

Ears of my old age;
The summer rains
   Falling down the rain-pipe.
            BUSON

One after another,
People rest on this stone
    On the summer moor.
        SHIKI

A fire-fly flitted by:
"Look!" I almost said,—
    But I was alone.
        TAIGI

Over my legs,
Stretched out at ease,
    The billowing clouds.
        ISSA

The old man
Hoeing the field,
    Has his hat on crooked.
        KITO

43

A horse tied
To a low tree,
　　In the summer moor.
　　　　　　SHIKI

The summer river;
In mid-stream,
　　Looking back.
　　　　　　SHIKI

Ah, summer grasses!
All that remains
　　Of the warriors' dreams.
　　　　　　BASHO

The peonies
Of the great garden,—
　　In a part of heaven.
　　　　　　BUSON

In the shade of the thicket,
A woman by herself,
Singing the planting-song.
ISSA

Encastled,
Three thousand warriors,—
These young leaves!
SHIKI

The morning after the storm;
The melons alone
Know nothing of it.
SODO

A boy
Getting a dog to run
Under the summer moon.
SHOHA

45

'Entering Autumn'

An autumn evening;
Without a cry,
   A crow passes.
               KISHU

Scooping up the moon
In the wash-basin,
   And spilling it.
               RYUHO

There are hamlets
That know not sea-beam or flowers,
   But all have today's moon.
               SAIKAKU

京都・三千院

gardens of the Sanzenin Shrine at Kyoto

Entering autumn,
The painting of flowering plants
A daily task.
SHIKI

An autumn evening;
A man on a journey
Sewing his clothes.
ISSA

An autumn eve;
She comes and asks,
"Shall I light the lamp?"
ETSUJIN

The bright autumn moon:
The shadows of tree and grass,—
And those of men!
BAISHITSU

A hundred different gourds,
From the mind
Of one vine.
CHIYO-NI

Sweeping them up,
And then not sweeping them,—
The falling leaves.
TAIGI

The wind of autumn
Blew first of all
Upon the morning-glories.
CHORA

Under a passage of wild geese,
Over the foot-hills,
A moon is signed.
BUSON

How beautiful,
After the autumn storm,
The red pepper.
BUSON

Autumn deepens;
Scarecrows are clad
In fallen leaves.
OTSUYU

The beginning of autumn;
What is the fortune-teller
Looking so surprised at?
BUSON

At meal-time, in autumn:
Through the open door,
The evening sun.
CHORA

A fine day of autumn;
Smoke from something
    Rises into the sky.
                SHIKI

Two houses,
The doors are open:
    The autumn mountains.
                MICHIHIKO

Bent over by the rain,
The ears of barley
    Make it a narrow path.
                JOSO

From far and near,
Voices of waterfalls are heard,
    Leaves falling.
                BASHO

Rain over the autumn moon:
Beneath the window,
Chestnuts pattering down.
USEN

It is seen
In the papier-mache cat,
This morning of autumn.
BASHO

The voice of the bell
Eddies through the mist,
In the morning twilight.
BASHO

The ferry-man's pole
Has been stolen away
By the autumn tempest.
BUSON

The slanting sun:
The shadow of a hill with a deer on it
Enters the temple gate.
BUSON

Along this road
Goes no one;
Autumn eve is falling.
BASHO

The moon swiftly fleeting,
Branches still holding
The rain-drops.
BASHO

From time to time
The clouds give rest
To the moon-beholders.
BASHO

The coolness:
The voice of the bell
    As it leaves the bell!
                BUSON

An autumn night;
Dreams, snores,
    The chirping of crickets.
                SUIO

Falling into the fields,
Falling from the fields,
    The water of autumn.
                BUSON

The autumn wind
Moved the scarecrow,
    And passed on.
                BUSON

宮島

an inland sea at Miyajima

Autumn's bright moon,
However far I walked, still afar off
    In an unknown sky.
                CHIYO-NI

The turnip-puller
Points the way
    With a turnip.
                ISSA

The young child,—
But when he laughed,—
    An autumn evening.
                ISSA

Millionaires
Come and drink of this clear water,
    And bears.
                SHIKI

White chrysanthemums!
Where is there a color
    So happy, so gracious?
            BUSON

On the mountain, day has closed;
On the moor, the pampas grass
    In the twilight.
            BUSON

Between the moon coming out
And the sun going in,—
    The red dragon-flies.
            NIKYU

In the misty rain,
The rose-mallows
    Make a bright sky.
            BASHO

Not yet having become a Buddha,
This ancient pine-tree,
    Idly dreaming.
                ISSA

I kept hanging the moon
On the pine-tree, and taking it off,
    Gazing at it the while.
                HOKUSHI

In the surf,
Mingled with small shells,
    Petals of the bush-clover.
                BASHO

The names unknown
But to every weed its flower,
    And loveliness.
                SAMPU

The white chrysanthemum;
Not a speck of dust
   To meet the eye.
           BASHO

The morning-glories;
In the faces of men
   There are faults.
           ISSA

I take a nap,
Making the mountain water
   Pound the rice.
           ISSA

Every year
Thinking of the chrysanthemums,
   Being thought of by them.
           SHIKI

A small shop,
Carving dolls;
    Chrysanthemum flowers.
        SHIKI

Wisps of my hair
Quiver together with the plumes
    Of the pampas grass.
        ISSA

After the dancing,
The wind in the pine-trees,
    The voices of insects.
        SOGETSU-NI

Foxes playing
Among the narcissus flowers,
    In the early evening moonlight.
        BUSON

Composed in Optima, a Roman face
of graceful simplicity, which embodies the spirit
of haiku poetry, designed by Hermann Zapf.
Set at the Castle Press by Grant Dahlstrom.
Printed on Hallmark Book Paper.
Japanese calligraphy by Nanae Ito.
Designed by Frances Yamashita.